COCKTAILS FOR THE HOLIDAYS

COCKTAILS
FOR THE
Holidays

FESTIVE DRINKS TO
CELEBRATE THE SEASON

BY THE EDITORS OF **imbibe** MAGAZINE

PHOTOGRAPHS BY LARA FERRONI

Library of Congress Cataloging-in-Publication Data available.

ISBN 978-1-4521-2782-8

Manufactured in China

Designed by Agnes Lee
Typesetting by DC Typography

10 9 8 7 6 5 4 3 2 1

Chronicle Books LLC
680 Second Street
San Francisco, California 94107
www.chroniclebooks.com

ACKNOWLEDGMENTS

Without the creativity of bartenders, the holidays wouldn't be nearly as festive, and this book wouldn't be so full of seasonal inspiration. Thank you to all of the incredibly talented bartenders who shared their recipes and expertise for this book, along with their own personal stories of holiday traditions, old and new.

CONTENTS

INTRODUCTION

Close your eyes and picture your favorite winter holiday. What sights, sounds, smells, and flavors fill your mind? Glasses clinking, corks popping, spices baking, cider simmering. It's a season of bounty, of giving, celebrating, sharing, and savoring. Thanksgiving, Hanukkah, Christmas, Kwanzaa, New Year's Eve—there's plenty to rejoice in all winter long, and what better way to do that than with a special cocktail in hand? That's, of course, where we come in.

We at *Imbibe* love the holidays—in fact, it's our favorite time of year. It's a time when we can savor classics like a Tom and Jerry, while also celebrating creative bartenders who dream up new recipes to highlight the best of the season, like a Cranberry Smash. Whether contemporary or classic, holiday cocktails are all about comfort, celebration, and, perhaps most important, enjoyment. Between shopping, cooking, and entertaining, there's a lot to manage during the holiday season, so we're here to make the drinks portion of your planning easy and stress free.

We've compiled recipes for all types of occasions, with ingredients that are easy to find or make, many of which you'll probably already have on hand during this time of the year. So whether you're hosting a party, organizing a dinner, or just looking for a drink to sip by a fire on a holiday eve, you'll find plenty of inspiration on the pages that follow. We've compiled fifty of our favorite new and classic recipes from some of the world's brightest bartenders, so whichever recipes you choose, you can't go wrong.

Dare we say that our job here is done? Now go forth, drink, and be merry.

Happy holidays!

TEAM *IMBIBE*

CHAPTER 1

CLASSICS,
New & Old

There's something comforting about a classic cocktail for the holidays. Eggnog, Tom and Jerry, mulled wine—these are the drinks that holiday traditions are made of. But in the cocktail world, there's always room for a twist. That's why we've compiled a group of cocktails that celebrate the spirit of the classics—those of yesteryear and those in the making (and a few modern twists on traditional recipes). Añejo Tequila and Amontillado Sherry Eggnog (page 33)? A Spiced Pear Daiquiri (page 21)? Irish Coffee (page 15)? It's time to raise a glass to the classics.

YULETIDE DAISY

The classic Daisy has inspired a good number of cocktails (Margarita, anyone?). This seasonal riff combines richly concentrated pomegranate flavors with citrus and simple syrup, while the vodka acts as the spirited glue that brings the ingredients together in wintertime harmony. "From the intensity of the pomegranate to the zip of the lime, each ingredient stands out on its own yet also works to complement the others," says Tampa bartender Dean Hurst.

TOOLS

cocktail shaker, strainer

GLASS

goblet or cocktail

GARNISH

lime wheel

1½ ounces vodka

½ ounce real pomegranate grenadine

½ ounce fresh lime juice

½ ounce Simple Syrup (recipe follows)

Ice cubes

 Combine the vodka, grenadine, lime juice, and simple syrup in a cocktail shaker and shake with ice. Strain into a chilled goblet and garnish with the lime wheel.

DEAN HURST
SIDEBERN'S, TAMPA, FLORIDA

TIP *This cocktail also works as a highball—simply shake the ingredients as described above and top with 2 ounces of club soda.*

SIMPLE SYRUP

MAKES ABOUT 1½ CUPS

1 cup water

1 cup granulated sugar

Combine the water and sugar in a small saucepan and bring to a boil over medium-high heat, stirring constantly. Turn the heat to medium-low and simmer, stirring slowly, until the sugar is dissolved, 2 to 3 minutes. Remove from the heat and let cool to room temperature. Transfer to a clean glass bottle, cover, and refrigerate for up to 2 weeks.

TUXEDO COCKTAIL

This relative of the Martini is an adaptation of a recipe from *Old Waldorf Bar Days* by Albert Stevens Crockett. It swaps vermouth's herbal character for the distinctive nuttiness of fino sherry, resulting in a distinctively dry cocktail that's perfect for serving alongside a holiday spread or as more of an aperitif before the feast begins. Since sherry is a staple ingredient of the holidays, this is a great recipe to keep on hand when you need to mix something that's easy, quick, and delicious.

2 ounces gin

1 ounce fino sherry

Dash of orange bitters

Ice cubes

Combine the gin, sherry, and bitters in a mixing glass. Add ice and stir until chilled. Strain into a chilled cocktail glass and garnish with the lemon twist.

IRISH COFFEE

Irishman Joseph Sheridan first invented this classic on a dreary night back in the 1940s to rouse tired, chilly travelers. Irish Coffee has since become a staple of bar menus around the world and a traditional recipe for the holiday season. It's a comforting blend of whiskey, coffee, brown sugar, and fresh cream, which makes the nippy evenings of the holiday season all the more cheerful.

6 ounces fresh-brewed coffee

1 tablespoon light brown sugar

1½ ounces Irish whiskey

3 tablespoons lightly whipped cream (see Tip)

Pour the hot coffee into a warmed Irish coffee glass. Stir in the brown sugar to dissolve. Pour in the whiskey and stir. Top the coffee by pouring the cream over the back of a spoon so that it floats. Garnish with the coffee bean.

TIP *The whipped cream should be pourable. Do not stir the drink after adding the cream, as the true flavor emerges by drinking the coffee and whiskey through it.*

SERVES

1

TOOLS

barspoon

GLASS

Irish coffee

GARNISH

roasted coffee bean

FAIRYTALE OF NEW YORK

An Old Fashioned is one of the most comforting cocktails of all, and the inspiration for this Canadian twist on the enduring classic. "The notes of spice, vanilla, and toffee from the whisky go nicely with the hint of orange, which pairs perfectly with the slight sweetness of the apple and pear syrup. And that touch of cinnamon and walnut from the bitters brings it all together and makes a damn good Canadian version of an Old Fashioned," says bartender Dave Mitton, who adds that every winter it's one of the most popular drinks at his Toronto bar, the Harbord Room.

SERVES

1

TOOLS

mixing glass, muddler, barspoon, strainer

GLASS

old-fashioned

1 piece of orange peel (about 1 by 2 inches)

¾ ounce Winter Warmth Syrup (page 18)

2 dashes of Fee Brothers black walnut bitters

2 ounces Canadian whisky (Mitton uses Forty Creek barrel select)

Ice cubes

Place the orange peel in the bottom of a mixing glass, pour in the syrup and bitters, and muddle together. Pour in the whisky, add ice cubes, and stir until well blended and chilled. Strain over 1 large ice cube in an old-fashioned glass.

DAVE MITTON
THE HARBORD ROOM, TORONTO, CANADA

WINTER WARMTH SYRUP

MAKES ABOUT 2 CUPS

1½ cups water

1 cup Demerara sugar

½ apple, peeled, cored, and diced

½ pear, peeled, cored, and diced

12 walnut halves

3 cinnamon sticks, broken up

6 whole cloves

1 whole nutmeg

Combine the water, sugar, apple, pear, walnuts, cinnamon sticks, cloves, and nutmeg in a medium saucepan over medium heat. Bring to a simmer, stirring until the sugar dissolves, and continue simmering for 10 to 20 minutes. Remove from the heat and let cool. Strain through a sieve to remove all the fruit, nuts, and spices. Transfer to a clean glass bottle, cover, and refrigerate for up to 2 weeks.

WHITECAP

This velvety rum punch is Jeff "Beach Bum" Berry's take on classic Hot Buttered Rum. "I wanted to serve guests a holiday-season tiki drink that would be a tropical alternative to the usual Hot Buttered Rum," says Berry. "Eventually I hit on the notion of using coconut cream instead of dairy butter. The other ingredients fell into place after that, with cloves and a cinnamon stick for garnish reinforcing the wintry taste profile." Just a few sips, and you'll be feeling as sun-soaked and relaxed as the Beach Bum himself.

SERVES

1

TOOLS

barspoon

GLASS

mug

GARNISH

cinnamon
stick

¾ ounce sweetened cream of
    coconut, such as Coco López

1 ounce 151-proof gold rum,
    such as Cruzan or Bacardi

½ ounce dark Jamaican rum

½ ounce light rum

3 whole cloves

8 ounces whole milk

Pinch of ground cinnamon

Combine the cream of coconut, the three rums, and the cloves in a warmed mug. In a small saucepan, bring the milk to a gentle boil. Pour the milk into the mug and stir. Top with the ground cinnamon and garnish with the cinnamon stick.

JEFF "BEACH BUM" BERRY
NEW ORLEANS, LOUISIANA

SPICED PEAR DAIQUIRI

Pears are a hallmark of the holiday season, and this cocktail from Chicago-based cocktail consultant Todd Appel fuses that earthy-sweet seasonal fruit with rhum agricole (a spirit distilled from fresh-pressed sugarcane juice), lemon juice, and a syrup chock-full of wintry warmth. About this cold-weather take on the classic Cuban daiquiri Appel says, "The blend of rhum, pear, spices, and lemon sits in perfect balance with all the flavors of the season."

2 ounces rhum agricole

½ ounce Spiced Simple Syrup
(page 22)

¾ ounce fresh lemon juice

1 ounce pear juice or pear purée
(see Tip)

Ice cubes

❄ Combine the rhum agricole, simple syrup, lemon juice, and pear juice in a cocktail shaker. Add ice and shake well. Strain into a chilled coupe and garnish with the pear slice.

TODD APPEL
CHICAGO, ILLINOIS

TIP *Appel uses Comice pears (also known as "Christmas pears" for their wintertime availability) to make his pear juice, but any juicy pear will work. If you don't have a juicer, core and roughly chop very soft, ripe pears and purée them in a blender. Strain the purée through a strainer lined with a double layer of cheesecloth. Gather the cheesecloth and squeeze all the liquid out. Or, if you want the simplest option, buy high-quality pear juice or purée; Appel's favorite is from Perfect Purée.*

SERVES

1

TOOLS

cocktail
shaker,
strainer

GLASS

coupe

GARNISH

fresh
pear slice,
lemon
twist, or
candied
lemon peel

SPICED SIMPLE SYRUP

MAKES ABOUT 2½ CUPS

2 cups granulated sugar

1½ cups water

¼ cup allspice berries

¼ cup whole cloves

2 cinnamon sticks

3 whole nutmegs

1 tablespoon whole black peppercorns

1 teaspoon vanilla extract

Combine the sugar, water, allspice, cloves, cinnamon sticks, nutmegs, and peppercorns in a medium saucepan over low heat. Stir just until the sugar dissolves, remove from the heat, and let cool to room temperature. Strain into a clean glass bottle, add the vanilla, and shake to combine. Cover and keep refrigerated for up to 3 weeks.

THE SPOTTED PIG'S MULLED WINE

SERVES

12 to 14

TOOLS

ladle

GLASS

punch cups
or mugs

GARNISH

orange
wheels

When snow falls in New York City, blanketing even the sharpest silhouette of a skyscraper in swathes of pillowy white, there is no cozier seat in town than a bar stool at the Spotted Pig. A never-ending stream of city dwellers and tourists alike keep it toasty and lively, and bartenders pour liquid warmth of all sorts, including their signature Mulled Wine, which has quickly become a modern classic. One sip of this spicy, citrus-laced libation will melt even the deepest chill. Mix up a batch of your own and warm your loved ones—and yourself—from the inside out.

4 (750-ml) bottles red wine

1 orange, sliced into wheels

½ lemon, sliced into wheels

4 cinnamon sticks

4 bay leaves

1 vanilla bean, split lengthwise and
 seeds scraped out (use both the
 pod and the seeds)

1 teaspoon whole black peppercorns

¾ teaspoon whole allspice berries

½ teaspoon red pepper flakes

2 cups superfine sugar

3 ounces Cognac

Combine the wine, orange and lemon wheels, cinnamon sticks, bay leaves, vanilla bean pod and seeds, peppercorns, allspice, red pepper flakes, and sugar in a large pot. Bring to a boil, stirring until the sugar dissolves. Remove from the heat and add the Cognac. Ladle into warmed punch cups. Garnish with the orange wheels.

APRIL BLOOMFIELD
THE SPOTTED PIG, NEW YORK, NEW YORK

TIP *Bloomfield recommends using four bottles of the same type of wine for this punch so that you don't have to worry about whether or not they will blend well. "It doesn't have to be anything fancy," she says. "Just something you would like to drink on its own." But she adds that it's not going to ruin the drink to use four different wines. She also emphasizes the importance of removing the mulled wine from the heat before adding the Cognac so you don't cook off all the alcohol.*

STINGER

While the Stinger's origins are shrouded in mystery, the cocktail has managed to maintain its standing among the most enduring classics. Highlighting two quintessentially wintry ingredients—Cognac and crème de menthe—it's a stunningly simple cocktail, packed with flavor and warming to the core. So when you're looking for a no-frills holiday recipe that's sure to impress, look no further than the steadfast Stinger.

SERVES

1

TOOLS

mixing glass, barspoon, strainer

GLASS

coupe or cocktail

2¼ ounces Cognac

Ice cubes

¾ ounce white crème de menthe

❄ Combine the Cognac and crème de menthe in a mixing glass, add ice, and stir until chilled. Strain into a chilled coupe.

TIP *In a cocktail this simple, the quality of your ingredients is critical, so be sure to use a high-quality Cognac and crème de menthe.*

AND TO ALL A GOOD NIGHT

SERVES

2

TOOLS

mixing glass, barspoon, strainer

GLASS

cordials

GARNISH

orange twists (optional)

We look forward to the holidays all year long, but once they arrive, it can be tough to find a moment to enjoy them. Think of this cheery cocktail as your little helper, a reminder to stop and savor. It's a perfect cocktail to sip after dinner and a drink so good you'll consider it an instant classic. "In creating this cocktail, I wanted to use Cherry Heering since it seems Christmassy with its strong fruit and musty flavors," says San Francisco bartender Tim Stookey. "Then I had to lighten it and start adding spice. I like the spiciness of reposado tequila, but I still needed more, so I added Regans' orange bitters. A dash of Angostura, and it was ready." So, when the last of the food has been gobbled and the final gift opened, mix up a few of these glowing little digestifs. Peace and joy, found.

1½ ounces bourbon

¾ ounce reposado tequila

¾ ounce Cherry Heering liqueur

2 dashes of Regans' orange bitters

Dash of Angostura bitters

Ice cubes

Combine the bourbon, tequila, Cherry Heering, and Regans' and Angostura bitters in a mixing glass filled with ice and stir until chilled. Strain into two cordial glasses and garnish with the orange twists, if desired.

TIM STOOKEY
THE PRESIDIO SOCIAL CLUB, SAN FRANCISCO, CALIFORNIA

TIP *To balance the spiciness of this cocktail, Stookey recommends using a bourbon with a sweeter flavor profile, such as Maker's Mark.*

ROB ROY'S TOM AND JERRY

If you love eggnog, then give its warming, wintry cousin the Tom and Jerry a go. Dating back to the mid-nineteenth century, this creation was once so popular that Tom and Jerry–emblazoned punch bowls and cups were all the rage; in fact, these punch sets still pop up in antiques stores throughout the holiday season. A mix of whipped eggs, sugar, spirit, and spice, Tom and Jerry is a cold-weather staple throughout the Midwest. In recent years the tradition has spread from coast to coast, including to Seattle's Rob Roy, where the house version makes an annual appearance as part of the bar's boozy advent calendar (a different season-ally inspired drink is offered each day throughout December).

2 ounces Tom and Jerry Batter (page 30)

1 ounce brandy

1 ounce aged rum

2 ounces hot milk

2 ounces hot water

❄ Combine the batter, brandy, rum, milk, and water in a mug and whisk or stir gently to blend.

ROB ROY, SEATTLE, WASHINGTON

TIP *Craving an extra-decadent drink? The Rob Roy crew is known to mix several shavings of black truffle into the batter and top each drink with a pinch of black truffle salt.*

TOM AND JERRY BATTER

MAKES ABOUT 4½ CUPS, ENOUGH FOR 18 TO 20 DRINKS

12 eggs, separated

2 cups granulated sugar

2 ounces aged rum

½ teaspoon ground cloves

½ teaspoon freshly grated nutmeg

½ teaspoon ground allspice

※ In a large mixing bowl, whisk the egg yolks until thin (you can use an electric mixer if you'd like). Gradually whisk in the sugar, then add the rum, cloves, nutmeg, and allspice. In a separate bowl, whisk the egg whites until stiff peaks form. Gently fold the egg whites into the yolk mixture until combined. You can make this ahead of time and refrigerate overnight.

SPICE NOG FLIP

Sometime you crave just a single serving of eggnog, which is where this recipe comes in. "With a splash of rum, some ice, and a quick trip to the fridge, you can easily shake this up," says Victoria, British Columbia, bartender Nate Caudle. Just don't forget the cinnamon and nutmeg. "They are called Christmas spices for a reason," he says, "and they really shine in this cocktail, which would make even Santa's cheeks just a tad rosier."

2 ounces black spiced rum

1 tablespoon powdered sugar

⅛ teaspoon freshly grated nutmeg

⅛ teaspoon ground cinnamon

2 ounces half-and-half

1 egg

Dash of vanilla extract

Ice cubes

Combine the rum, powdered sugar, nutmeg, cinnamon, half-and-half, egg, and vanilla in a cocktail shaker. Add ice and shake well. Double strain into a chilled mug and garnish with a dusting of nutmeg and the cinnamon stick.

NATE CAUDLE
LITTLE JUMBO, VICTORIA, BRITISH COLUMBIA

TIP *Afraid of egg cocktails? Don't be! Eggs add voluptuous viscosity to cocktails, amplifying flavors from both spirit and spice. Just be sure to shake the drink hard with ice to allow the egg to fully incorporate into the drink.*

SERVES

1

TOOLS

cocktail shaker, strainer, fine-mesh strainer

GLASS

mug or punch cup

GARNISH

freshly grated nutmeg and a cinnamon stick

AÑEJO TEQUILA AND AMONTILLADO SHERRY EGGNOG

SERVES

about
10

TOOLS

blender
or stand
mixer

GLASS

punch cups

GARNISH

freshly
grated
nutmeg

Every winter during the holidays, Clyde Common bar manager Jeffrey Morgenthaler's eggnog makes its seasonal appearance, and it's like no other eggnog you've ever tasted. Instead of incorporating traditional eggnog spirits, such as whiskey, rum, or Cognac, Morgenthaler opts for a base of tequila and sherry for a nog that's subtly spicy, warming, and utterly unique. "My idea was to do a rotating daily or weekly eggnog during the holidays with unique spirits and liqueurs or fortified wines," says Morgenthaler. "The first one I tried was with añejo tequila and amontillado sherry, and it was so popular right off the bat—insanely popular. We've been serving it ever since."

6 eggs

1 cup plus 2 tablespoons
    granulated sugar

1½ teaspoons freshly grated nutmeg

2¼ cups whole milk

12 ounces heavy cream

7½ ounces amontillado sherry

6 ounces añejo tequila

In a blender or stand mixer on low speed, blend or beat the eggs until smooth. Slowly add the sugar and nutmeg, blending until incorporated and the sugar has dissolved. Slowly add the milk, cream, sherry, and tequila, blending until combined. Refrigerate for at least 3 hours or overnight. Serve in chilled punch cups and garnish with a dusting of nutmeg.

JEFFREY MORGENTHALER
CLYDE COMMON, PORTLAND, OREGON

TIP *Morgenthaler advises not running your blender on too high a speed when you're beating the eggs; otherwise you run the risk of scrambling them.*

CHAPTER 2

Winter WARMERS

❄

Spent the day dashing through the snow? Come in from the cold and blanket yourself with some of our favorite winter warmers. Whether you're settling in for a quiet evening with friends or taking a quick break from the powder-kissed slopes, these mugs will make you merrier with every sip. From the boozy Dutch Cocoa (page 37) to the Scotch-spiked Highland Toddy (page 39) to the applejack-bolstered Hot Buttered Cider (page 51), these comforting drinks warm to the core. So come in from the cold and cozy up with a cocktail.

DUTCH COCOA

While powdery snow dances to the ground outside, inside we keep cozy with this comforting cup of spiked cocoa from Portland, Oregon, bartender Brandon Wise. "The ingredients all work in such harmony," says Wise, noting that the genever introduces subtle maltiness; Chartreuse lends an herbaceous complexity and rich aromatics; and the triple sec helps bring everything together and round out the flavors. "It's an anytime drink during the holidays," Wise adds, "perfectly suited for caroling, raucous holiday parties, or watching the snowflakes descend from the heavens."

5 ounces freshly made
    hot chocolate

1 ounce genever

¼ ounce green Chartreuse
    (see Tip, page 42)

¼ ounce triple sec

Combine the hot chocolate, genever, Chartreuse, and triple sec in a mug and stir gently to combine. Garnish liberally with Chartreuse Whipped Cream and top with chocolate curls, if desired.

BRANDON WISE
IMPERIAL AND PENNY DINER, PORTLAND, OREGON

SERVES

1

TOOLS

barspoon

GLASS

mug

GARNISH

Chartreuse Whipped Cream (page 38) and chocolate curls (optional)

CHARTREUSE WHIPPED CREAM

MAKES ABOUT ½ CUP

¼ cup heavy whipping cream

½ ounce green Chartreuse

1 teaspoon granulated sugar

 Whisk together the heavy cream, Chartreuse, and sugar in a small bowl until soft peaks form. Refrigerate for up to 1 week.

HIGHLAND TODDY

Sure, a warming mug of Earl Grey can soothe, but one spiked with Scotch and ginger? Now *that* is our cup of tea. Taking its inspiration from the blustery hills of Scotland, this toddy from Wisconsin bartender Samuel Gauthier wraps you in a wintry cloak of peaty Scotch, bergamot-soaked tea, and spicy fresh ginger. "I was going for something that offered both holiday comfort and an invigorating brightness," says Gauthier. "It's the kind of winter warmer you'd want to drink on a cold Highland night."

2 ounces Scotch

⅓ ounce Simple Syrup (page 13)

3 dashes of Angostura bitters

4 ounces hot Earl Grey tea

2 quarter-sized rounds fresh ginger, peeled

❄ Combine the Scotch, simple syrup, bitters, tea, and ginger in an Irish coffee glass and stir to combine. Garnish with candied ginger, if desired.

SAMUEL GAUTHIER
MERCHANT, MADISON, WISCONSIN

(TIP) *Adjust the sweetness by adding more or less simple syrup, or by swapping in alternative sweeteners, such as honey or agave syrup.*

SERVES

1

TOOLS

barspoon

GLASS

Irish coffee

GARNISH

candied ginger (optional)

FERNET-APPLE TODDY

Got a case of the sniffles this holiday season? Grandma swore by the restorative powers of a soothing hot toddy, and this winter warmer from Portland, Oregon–based Douglas Derrick fuses that cold-weather classic with hot apple cider, Angostura bitters, and a nip of herbal Fernet-Branca. "It's my go-to after a cold kicks in," Derrick says. "But it's soothing no matter what state your health is in." Though we can't promise it will cure what ails you, we guarantee you'll have a delicious time drinking it!

3 ounces fresh apple cider

½ ounce fresh lemon juice

½ ounce honey syrup (see Note)

1¾ ounces aged rum

⅓ ounce Fernet-Branca

2 dashes of Angostura bitters

In a small saucepan, heat the cider, lemon juice, and honey syrup to a simmer. Remove from the heat and stir in the rum, Fernet-Branca, and bitters. Pour into a warm mug and garnish with the orange wheel studded with cloves.

NOTE To make the honey syrup, stir together 2¼ teaspoons of honey and ¾ teaspoon of warm water.

DOUGLAS DERRICK
PORTLAND, OREGON

SERVES

1

TOOLS

barspoon

GLASS

mug or toddy

GARNISH

orange wheel studded with cloves

PEARL STREET WARMER

Our favorite part of a festive feast? Dessert. And this subtly sweet, coffee-fueled sipper is a delicious accompaniment to any after-dinner spread. Balancing a whiskey-spiked jolt with the digestive properties of an ancient herbal French liqueur, the drink gets a dollop of honey-sweetened Whiskey Whipped Cream. The whipped cream also makes a decadent dessert topper for seasonal favorites like pecan pie, apple crisp, and the classic Yule log.

2 ounces strong fresh-brewed coffee

1½ ounces rye whiskey

½ ounce yellow Chartreuse (see Tip)

½ ounce honey syrup (2:1; see Note)

※ Combine the coffee, whiskey, Chartreuse, and honey syrup in a warm mug and stir to blend. Top with a heaping spoonful of whipped cream and a dusting of nutmeg.

(NOTE) To make the honey syrup, stir together 2 teaspoons of honey and 1 teaspoon of warm water.

BRYAN DALTON
OAK AT FOURTEENTH, BOULDER, COLORADO

(TIP) *Chartreuse—also known as "the elixir of long life"—is an herbal liqueur that dates back to 1605. Made by Carthusian monks with more than 125 herbs and botanicals, its recipe is protected under a vow of silence. Chartreuse comes in both a green and yellow style. The green is more assertive and spicy, while the yellow is subtler with a soft honeyed sweetness. It's delicious in this coffee cocktail, mixed into a brandy hot toddy, or simply splashed into a hot cup of tea.*

WHISKEY WHIPPED CREAM

MAKES ABOUT 2 CUPS

2 ounces rye whiskey

1½ teaspoons honey syrup (see Note)

1 cup heavy whipping cream

❄ In a medium mixing bowl, combine the whiskey, honey syrup, and cream. Whip with a wire whisk until soft peaks form. Refrigerate for up to 1 week.

(NOTE) To make the honey syrup, stir together 1 teaspoon of honey and ½ teaspoon of warm water.

WINTER JULEP

If you thought juleps were only for the summer months, think again. Atlanta bartender Lara Creasy wanted to find a way to transform the classic hot-weather cocktail to a warming drink for the colder months. After a bit of tinkering, she found that peppermint tea was a perfect base for a good pour of bourbon, and the Winter Julep was born. Between the candy canes that hang from the tree and the starlight candies that line the roofs of gingerbread houses, who doesn't crave mint all December long? Let the kids keep their candy canes and have yourself this properly grown-up treat.

SERVES

1

TOOLS

tea infuser, barspoon

GLASS

heat-proof brandy snifter or Irish coffee

GARNISH

mint sprig (see Tip)

1 teaspoon peppermint tea leaves

5 ounces boiling water

1½ ounces bourbon

¾ ounce brown sugar syrup (see Note)

❄ In a warm heat-proof brandy snifter, use an infuser to steep the tea leaves in the boiling water for 4 minutes. Remove the infuser. Add the bourbon and brown sugar syrup and stir to combine. Garnish with the mint sprig.

(NOTE) To make the brown sugar syrup, in a small cup, combine 1⅛ teaspoons of brown sugar with 1⅛ teaspoons of boiling water. Stir to dissolve the sugar and allow to cool.

LARA CREASY
FOUR 28, ATLANTA, GEORGIA

(TIP) *Creasy never puts the fresh mint garnish directly into the drink. "I prefer to garnish on the side, especially if using a saucer to serve the warm mug on. Just lay the mint to the side of the mug."*

SERVES

1

TOOLS

barspoon

GLASS

10-ounce
heat-proof
glass or
mug

GARNISH

Cinnamon
Whipped
Cream
(recipe
follows)

IN LIKE A LION

Memories of family traditions inspired this wintry recipe from Virginia bartender Michelle Shriver, who combines a quartet of warming ingredients and tops them with a spiced whipped cream for extra indulgence. "There are so many traditions and family memories connected with the food and drink of the holiday season," says Shriver. "My mother's Dutch heritage was reflected in our food and family customs. A typical winter warmer for us children when we were under the weather was a hot beverage with strong spices like caraway, cinnamon, allspice, and a dash of liquor to soothe us—comfort in a glass."

1 ounce aquavit

½ ounce vodka

½ ounce maple syrup

6 ounces strong fresh-brewed coffee

Combine the aquavit, vodka, and maple syrup in a heat-proof glass. Stir to combine. Add the hot coffee and top with whipped cream.

MICHELLE SHRIVER
DUTCH & COMPANY, RICHMOND, VIRGINIA

CINNAMON WHIPPED CREAM

MAKES ABOUT 1 CUP

½ cup heavy whipping cream

¼ teaspoon ground cinnamon

⅛ teaspoon powdered sugar

Pinch of salt

In a medium mixing bowl, combine the heavy cream, cinnamon, powdered sugar, and salt. Whisk until soft peaks form. Refrigerate for up to 1 week.

 Shriver notes this whipped cream is richer and more savory than the usual sweet whipped cream.

WARM THOUGHTS

The smell of a holiday ham cooking was enough to inspire this toasty toddy from L.A. bartender Max Kestenbaum. "One day my mom was cooking an apple-cinnamon ham, and I walked into the kitchen and said to myself, 'I'm putting that in a cocktail!'" he recalls. "I knew right off the bat I was going to sauté apples and cinnamon in butter, shake it with rye, and serve it like a hot toddy." Consider it the perfect thing to sip while you're prepping your own holiday meal.

1 tablespoon Sautéed Apples
 (recipe follows)

2½ ounces rye whiskey

2 ounces hot water

½ ounce honey (or to taste)

❄ Muddle the sautéed apples in a cocktail shaker. Add the whiskey and shake. Set aside. Pour the hot water into a warm mug. Double strain the apple-whiskey mixture into the mug. Stir in the honey and garnish with the lemon slice.

MAX KESTENBAUM
APARTMENT A, LOS ANGELES, CALIFORNIA

SAUTÉED APPLES

MAKES 2 CUPS

2 tablespoons unsalted butter

2 Fuji apples, peeled, cored, and
 cut into small cubes

2 cinnamon sticks, broken up

❄ Melt the butter in a small skillet over medium heat. Add the apples and cinnamon and sauté for about 7 minutes, or until the apples are golden brown.

SERVES

1

TOOLS

muddler,
cocktail
shaker,
strainer,
fine-mesh
strainer,
barspoon

GLASS

mug

GARNISH

lemon slice

SERVES

1

GLASS

heat-proof
rocks

GARNISH

apple slice

THE SPICED APPLE

Crazy for apple pie? Then you'll love this boozy reinterpretation from Miami bartender Robert Ortenzio, which mixes spiced-apple goodness with bourbon and Chardonnay. "The infused bourbon provides the flavors of mulling spices, while the Chardonnay gives you the subtle taste of pastry crust," says Ortenzio. "A little bitters brings out the apple and ties it all together." The spiced bourbon infuses in a day and is itself a seasonal staple you'll want on hand all winter long. Try it splashed into freshly whipped cream or serve it solo after a rich meal.

1¼ ounces Spiced Apple Bourbon
(facing page)

¾ ounce Chardonnay

½ ounce fresh apple cider

½ ounce Cinnamon Syrup (page 65)
or Toasted Cinnamon Syrup
(page 78)

3 dashes of orange bitters

❄ Combine the bourbon, Chardonnay, cider, cinnamon syrup, and bitters in a small saucepan and heat until warm, stirring often. Pour into a heat-proof rocks glass and garnish with the apple slice.

ROBERT ORTENZIO
MIAMI, FLORIDA

(TIP) *This drink also works great chilled. Instead of heating all the ingredients, simply shake them with ice, and then strain into an ice-filled rocks glass.*

SPICED APPLE BOURBON

MAKES 4½ CUPS

4 Gala apples

1 (1-liter) bottle bourbon

2 whole star anise

4 whole cloves

6 cinnamon sticks

Core each apple and cut into 8 pieces. Transfer to a glass jar that is large enough to hold all the ingredients. Pour in the bourbon and add the star anise, cloves, and cinnamon sticks. Cover and let rest at room temperature for 24 hours. Strain into a clean glass bottle, cover, and store at room temperature for up to 1 month.

HOT BUTTERED CIDER

Every winter, New York bartender Naren Young turns to his go-to recipe for holiday gatherings. Combining spirits, lemon juice, maple syrup, apple cider, plenty of seasonal spices, and a dab of butter for good measure, it's a perfectly festive cross between a spiked cider and a hot buttered rum. "Using hard spices is perfect around the holidays, and serving something hot is always an amazing welcome to guests as they walk in the door," says Young. "Plus, it makes the whole house smell delicious."

6⅓ cups fresh apple cider

12 ounces applejack

2 ounces St-Germain elderflower liqueur

2 ounces amaretto

2 ounces fresh lemon juice

1 ounce maple syrup

2 cinnamon sticks

3 whole star anise

1 whole clove

¼ teaspoon freshly grated nutmeg

½ vanilla bean, split lengthwise and seeds scraped out (use both the pod and the seeds)

Combine the cider, applejack, St-Germain, amaretto, lemon juice, maple syrup, cinnamon sticks, star anise, clove, nutmeg, and vanilla bean pod and seeds in a large pot, stirring to blend. Bring to a low boil and remove from the heat. Ladle into heated teacups. Add a small dab of butter and a dusting of ground cinnamon to each cup.

NAREN YOUNG
EMPELLON, NEW YORK CITY

TIP *If you don't happen to have applejack on hand, Young says bourbon works just as well.*

SERVES

about

12

TOOLS

ladle

GLASS

teacups or toddies

GARNISH

unsalted butter and ground cinnamon

CINNAMON-CAMPARI SIDECAR

SERVES

about
10

TOOLS

ladle

GLASS

punch cups
or mugs

GARNISH

orange
twists
(optional)

"I wanted to create a seasonal drink, complex in flavor, that, once made, guests could serve themselves," says San Francisco bartender Duggan McDonnell of this recipe. It's full of festive flavor and can easily serve a large group, so it's perfect for a holiday party, where guests can ladle out their own servings. "The recipe is just a guideline, because as Jerry Thomas said in his classic nineteenth-century book, *The Bar-Tender's Guide*, 'Scarcely two persons make punch alike.'"

3 cups Calvados

8 ounces Campari

6¼ ounces falernum liqueur

2 cups granulated sugar

6 cinnamon sticks

¼ cup whole cloves

¼ cup whole star anise

12 ounces water

5 ounces fresh lemon juice

5 ounces fresh lime juice

3 ounces fresh orange juice

Peels of 2 oranges, cut into
long strands

Combine the Calvados, Campari, falernum liqueur, sugar, cinnamon sticks, cloves, star anise, and water in a large pot. Bring to a simmer over medium heat, stirring to dissolve the sugar. Lower the heat and simmer for about 4 hours (adjusting the sugar and water to taste, if needed), taking care not to let the mixture boil. Add the lemon, lime, and orange juices and stir to combine. Add the orange peels. Keep on low heat until you're ready to serve. Ladle into punch cups and garnish each serving with an orange twist, if you like.

DUGGAN MCDONNELL
CANTINA, SAN FRANCISCO, CALIFORNIA

CHAPTER 3

Party PUNCHES

If your holiday household is anything like ours, a small gathering can snowball into a full-blown fête in no time. Thankfully, our winter preparedness kit contains a cache of punch recipes, from the ultra-elegant Santa Clara Christmas (page 63), to the warm and soothing Honey Milk Punch (page 59), to the bright and cheery Vixen (page 57). You, too, can become holiday reveler–ready. Prep a festive punch that streamlines your shopping list (say good-bye to stocking a full bar). And since you won't need to spend as much time mixing drinks, you'll have more time for mingling—it's your party, after all! So fill the punch bowl, gather some friends, and get ready for your most inspired seasonal soirée yet.

VIXEN

Necessity is indeed the mother of invention. When asked what sparked the invention of this vibrantly colored punch, Ryan Goodspeed responded instantly, "Mediocre, watery cranberry juice." During the holiday season, poor-quality cranberry juice too often ruins an otherwise excellent cocktail, so Goodspeed set out to make his own. It's a breeze to put together, dazzles with tartness, and entices with a wintery perfume of fresh rosemary. Bitter Aperol and a touch of simple syrup and lemon tie the satin bow on this festive recipe.

SERVES

12 to **16**

TOOLS

large pitcher, punch bowl

GLASS

rocks

GARNISH

fresh cranberries and lemon wheels

3 cups vodka

12 ounces Rosemary-Infused Cranberry Juice (page 58)

8 ounces Aperol (see Tip)

4 ounces Simple Syrup (page 13)

2 ounces fresh lemon juice

Ice cubes

2 cups soda water (optional)

❄ Combine the vodka, cranberry juice, Aperol, simple syrup, and lemon juice in a large pitcher and refrigerate until well chilled. Pour over ice cubes into a punch bowl and stir. Add the soda water, if desired. Float fresh cranberries and lemon wheels as garnishes.

RYAN GOODSPEED
THE CYPRESS ROOM, MIAMI, FLORIDA

(TIP) *Aperol—a bittersweet Italian aperitif flavored with orange, rhubarb, gentian, and cinchona bark—is closely related to another jewel-toned mixer, Campari. And though the two share similarities in color and ingredients, Aperol is a tad sweeter, and comes in at about half the alcohol content.*

ROSEMARY-INFUSED CRANBERRY JUICE

MAKES ABOUT 8 CUPS

4 (12-ounce) bags frozen cranberries   10 sprigs fresh rosemary

8 cups water

❄ Combine the cranberries with 4 cups of the water in a large pot. Cook over medium-high heat, stirring frequently so as not to burn the fruit. When the cranberries soften and become mushy, add the remaining 4 cups water and the rosemary. Bring the mixture to a boil, remove from the heat, and let cool for 15 minutes. Strain the juice into a clean glass bottle, discarding the berries and rosemary. Cover and refrigerate for up to 2 weeks.

HONEY MILK PUNCH

What's more soothing than a warm cup of milk? Try one sweetened with honey and spiked with Scotch. Taking a cue from the classic Hot Milk Punch of the 1860s, Manhattan barman Dan Greenbaum updates the winter warmer by swapping in honey for the sugar. "Honey and milk work together beautifully," he says, "giving this punch its silky texture." A word of caution from Greenbaum: "A few mugs will sneak up on you fast!"

4 cups whole milk

2 cups blended Scotch (see Tip)

8 ounces honey syrup (see Note)

❄ Combine the milk, Scotch, and honey syrup in a medium saucepan and heat over medium-low heat, stirring frequently. When hot, ladle into teacups and garnish with a dusting of nutmeg.

(NOTE) To make the honey syrup, stir together ⅔ cup of honey and ⅓ cup of warm water.

DAN GREENBAUM
NEW YORK, NEW YORK

(TIP) *No Scotch on hand? This steamy sipper also works with rum, bourbon, or brandy.*

Greenbaum stresses the importance of heating the mixture slowly and never letting it come to a boil, as this could curdle the milk. Once it's warm, consider transferring it to a slow cooker set to low to keep it warm without overcooking.

SERVES

8 to 12

TOOLS

ladle

GLASS

teacups or mugs

GARNISH

freshly grated nutmeg

SERVES

4 or **5**

TOOLS

blender,
pitcher

GLASS

juice

GARNISH

freshly
grated
nutmeg

MACLEOD BREAKFAST PUNCH

A soft spot for an alcohol-free drink called a London Fog—Earl Grey tea with steamed milk and a bit of vanilla—led bartender Michael Phillips to develop this punch. "It dawned on me that the London Fog was akin to a classic Milk Punch, so I created a hybrid," he says. Phillips uses blended Scotch to complement the heady, citrus-and-floral notes of the Earl Grey, while a well-balanced cream blend and a whisper of vanilla round out the frothy drink—just the thing to sip on a quiet Christmas Eve at home.

2 Earl Grey tea bags

6 ounces boiling water

9 ounces Scotch

9 ounces cream blend (see Note)

2 ounces Vanilla Syrup (facing page)

1 egg white (see Tip)

In a large mug, steep the tea bags in the boiling water for 4 to 5 minutes. Remove the tea bags and pour the tea into a container with a lid. Cover and refrigerate until cool. Pour the tea, Scotch, cream blend, vanilla syrup, and egg white into a blender and blend for 10 seconds. Pour into a pitcher for serving. As you serve, lightly grate nutmeg on the froth in each glass.

NOTE To make the cream blend, stir together ¾ cup of half-and-half and ¼ cup plus 2 tablespoons of whole milk. Refrigerate for up to 1 day.

MICHAEL PHILLIPS
MIDNIGHT COWBOY, AUSTIN, TEXAS

TIP *Fresh egg whites will give you the best froth, but they are also the most diffi-cult to separate from the yolks. To separate them, crack the egg over a small bowl and pass the yolk between the eggshell halves, allowing the egg white to fall into the bowl. The white should be fairly bulbous and heavy. If the white slips out of the shell almost immediately, the egg is not at peak freshness, and you can add another egg white to help achieve the proper frothiness in the drink.*

VANILLA SYRUP

MAKES ABOUT ½ CUP

½ cup Demerara sugar

½ cup boiling water

½ teaspoon vanilla extract

❄ In a heat-proof bowl, stir together the Demerara sugar and boiling water. Add the vanilla and stir. Cool and transfer to a clean glass bottle, cover, and refrigerate for up to 2 weeks.

TIP *If you don't feel like making homemade vanilla syrup, a store-bought version will work just fine. B.G. Reynolds makes a great one.*

SANTA CLARA CHRISTMAS

This festive punch from Nashville bartender Alan Kennedy combines equal parts blanco tequila, aged mezcal, yellow Chartreuse, and sweet vermouth for a party-ready punch that can be easily multiplied for any number of holiday revelers. "From the warmth of the tequila to the spice of Chartreuse to the smoke of mezcal," says Kennedy, "each sip reminds me of sitting in front of a fire with all the winter spices in the air."

SERVES

8

TOOLS

large pitcher, strainer

GLASS

coupes

GARNISH

orange twists

6 ounces blanco tequila

6 ounces reposado mezcal

6 ounces yellow Chartreuse
(see Tip, page 42)

6 ounces sweet vermouth

Ice cubes

 Combine the tequila, mezcal, Chartreuse, and vermouth in a pitcher. Add ice and stir. Strain into chilled coupes and garnish each drink with an orange twist.

ALAN KENNEDY
MUSIC CITY TIPPLER, NASHVILLE, TENNESSEE

MIEL PICANTE PUNCH

Looking to heat things up this holiday season? This party punch from Manhattan bartender Jane Danger packs some added warmth with a jalapeño-and-rum honey. But chile-phobes shouldn't fear, the heat of the spiced honey is not at all overwhelming. "It's very light and warming," Danger notes, "and is the perfect combination of sweetness and spice."

6 ounces aged rum

12 ounces fresh apple cider

2 ounces fresh lemon juice

3 ounces Jalapeño-Rum Honey
(recipe follows)

Combine the rum, cider, lemon juice, and honey in a medium saucepan or a small slow cooker and heat until steaming. Ladle into mugs and garnish each serving with a dusting of cinnamon and a lemon wedge.

JANE DANGER
NEW YORK, NEW YORK

JALAPEÑO-RUM HONEY

MAKES ABOUT 1¾ CUPS

1½ cups honey

1 jalapeño, coarsely chopped
(seeds optional; see Tip)

2 ounces aged rum

Combine the honey, jalapeño, and rum in a small bowl. Stir, cover, and let sit overnight at room temperature. Strain the mixture into a clean jar to remove the jalapeño chunks. Cover and refrigerate for up to 1 month.

 If you're still intimidated by the potential heat from a jalapeño, halve the chile pepper and discard the seeds before chopping. Also, the leftover Jalapeño-Rum Honey is a great accompaniment to a holiday spread—spoon it over oven-fresh rolls and warm biscuits.

POWDER BURNS PUNCH

SERVES

15 to **20**

TOOLS

large pitcher, punch bowl, ladle

GLASS

punch cups

GARNISH

lemon wheels and cinnamon sticks

Whether you're giving an ugly-sweater party or a family feast, this big batch of punch will keep your holiday crowd in high spirits. Combining bourbon, bitters, and two liqueurs with cinnamon and citrus and fizzy seltzer, it has all the ingredients for a night of festive fun. All you have to do is send out the invitations.

1 (750-ml) bottle bourbon

9 ounces Cinnamon Syrup (recipe follows)

6 ounces Grand Marnier

2 ounces green Chartreuse (see Tip, page 42)

24 dashes of Angostura bitters

15 ounces filtered water

1 large block of ice

9 ounces fresh lemon juice

9 ounces fresh grapefruit juice

15 ounces cold seltzer water

❄ Up to 1 day ahead of time, combine the bourbon, cinnamon syrup, Grand Marnier, Chartreuse, bitters, and filtered water in a large pitcher and refrigerate. About 15 minutes before serving, put the block of ice in a punch bowl and add the chilled liquor mixture. Add the lemon and grapefruit juices and seltzer, gently stirring to combine. Ladle into punch cups and garnish with the lemon wheels and cinnamon sticks.

COLIN SHEARN
EL CAMINO, LOUISVILLE, KENTUCKY

CINNAMON SYRUP

MAKES ABOUT 1½ CUPS

1 cup granulated sugar

1 cup water

4 cinnamon sticks, broken into large pieces

❄ In a medium saucepan, bring the sugar, water, and cinnamon sticks to a boil. Reduce the heat to medium-low and simmer for 8 to 10 minutes, stirring frequently. Remove from the heat and let cool to room temperature. Strain into a clean glass bottle, cover, and refrigerate for up to 2 weeks.

YULETIDE WAVE

At first glance, drinks that call to mind sun and sand may seem out of place around the holidays, but Martin Cate, of San Francisco's rum-centric Smuggler's Cove, thinks they're a perfect fit. "Tiki drinks tend to use spices and flavors that are traditional in the United States for holiday baking, so it seems natural to start there," he says. Here, allspice and vanilla mingle with the bright zing of lemon and pineapple, while the addition of pear liqueur lends a hint of seasonal fruit. As for the drink's unique combination of rum and bourbon? "That was how my mother-in-law used to make a particularly brutal family eggnog recipe," Cate adds.

15 ounces pineapple juice

7½ ounces fresh lemon juice

5 ounces vanilla syrup, homemade (see page 61) or store-bought

10 ounces bourbon

10 ounces aged rum

5 ounces pear liqueur

2½ ounces allspice dram

Large pieces of ice (see Tip)

❄ Combine the pineapple juice, lemon juice, vanilla syrup, bourbon, rum, pear liqueur, and allspice dram in a pitcher and stir to combine. Cover and refrigerate for at least 4 hours. Place several pieces of ice in a punch bowl, pour in the punch, and stir. Sprinkle ground cinnamon over the surface and serve in punch cups, placing a cinnamon stick in each, if desired.

MARTIN CATE
SMUGGLER'S COVE, SAN FRANCISCO, CALIFORNIA

TIP *Cate says it's important to prep this punch in advance and make sure it gets nice and cold before serving. For the ice, he likes to use several jagged pieces about as big as a fist, rather than one block. To get these, freeze water in a couple of loaf pans. When the ice is ready, use an ice pick to chisel off some chunks.*

SERVES

10

TOOLS

large pitcher, barspoon, punch bowl

GLASS

punch cups

GARNISH

ground cinnamon and cinnamon sticks (optional)

SERVES

16 to **18**

TOOLS

punch
bowl,
barspoon

GLASS

punch cups

GARNISH

freshly
grated
nutmeg

SILK CITY PUNCH

In creating his ideal holiday punch, bartender Sean Kenyon looked back in time to Fish House Punch. "I've always used it as a basis for punches," he says. "It follows the classic formula: one part sour, two parts sweet, three parts strong, four parts weak." Here, Kenyon sticks with that formula, summoning an orchestra of bold flavors, from the deep, warming richness of rye whiskey and aged rum to aromatic lemon and bergamot. Strong, supremely balanced, and just a touch exotic, this punch is one your guests will remember.

2½ cups rye whiskey

10 ounces aged rum

10 ounces peach brandy

12 ounces fresh lemon juice

12 ounces Oleo Saccharum
(facing page)

5 cups brewed Earl Grey tea, cooled

1 large block of ice

Combine the whiskey, rum, brandy, lemon juice, Oleo Saccharum, and tea in a punch bowl with the large block of ice and stir to blend. Grate nutmeg over the surface and serve in punch cups.

SEAN KENYON
WILLIAMS & GRAHAM, DENVER, COLORADO

OLEO SACCHARUM

MAKES ABOUT 1¼ CUPS

6 lemons   1 cup superfine sugar

 Remove the zest from the lemons with a vegetable peeler and juice the lemons. Refrigerate the juice in a covered container. Combine the zest and sugar in a large jar or nonreactive container. Cover and let the mixture sit overnight at room temperature. When you're ready to make the punch, add the lemon juice to the peel-and-sugar mixture. Stir together, then strain out the peels.

TIP *Alternatively, the Oleo Saccharum can be made the same day as the punch. Simply add the lemon peels to the sugar and muddle them together. Let sit for 2 hours and then add the lemon juice. Stir to combine, then strain out the peels.*

SANTA'S LITTLE HELPER

Cinnamon, spice, and everything nice—that's what you'll find in this winter punch from Chicago barman Stephen Cole. "Clove and cinnamon are natural flavors for the holiday season," he says, "and the Angostura bitters, apple cider, and sweet vermouth really echo those notes." Best of all? It's simple and unfussy—just combine all the ingredients in a slow cooker, heat, and serve.

SERVES

12 to 15

TOOLS

slow cooker, ladle

GLASS

punch cups or mugs

GARNISH

orange twists, cinnamon sticks

1 (750-ml) bottle rye whiskey

1 (750-ml) bottle sweet vermouth (Cole uses Carpano Antica)

1 (1-gallon) jug fresh apple cider

3 cinnamon sticks

5 whole cloves

½ cup granulated sugar

10 dashes of Angostura bitters

Combine the whiskey, vermouth, cider, cinnamon sticks, cloves, sugar, and bitters in a slow cooker set to low and leave for 1 hour. I adle into punch cups and garnish each drink with an orange twist twirled around or pierced with a cinnamon stick.

STEPHEN COLE
BARRELHOUSE FLAT, CHICAGO, ILLINOIS

TIP *Is the slow cooker already in use? To heat on the stovetop instead, combine the ingredients in a large saucepan over medium-high heat until simmering, stirring occasionally. Ladle into mugs and garnish.*

SERVES

12 to 14

TOOLS

punch
bowl,
barspoon

GLASS

punch cups

GARNISH

orange
or lemon
wheels

MAXWELL HEIGHTS

Barman Jeremiah Blake named this recipe for a historic neighborhood in Nashville. "I love the communal aspect of punch," he says. This cocktail is attention-grabbing from the first sip, with powerful flavors like applejack and Curaçao. While you sip, the drink continues to unfold as subtle spices from the black tea syrup and the almond extract slowly emerge.

12 ounces applejack

12 ounces aged rum

3 ounces sweet vermouth

3 ounces orange Curaçao

11 ounces fresh lemon juice

11 ounces Orange-Spice Black Tea Syrup (facing page)

1 teaspoon almond extract

1 large ice ring (see "The Big Chill," page 110)

1 (750-ml bottle) cold sparkling wine

Combine the applejack, rum, vermouth, Curaçao, lemon juice, tea syrup, and almond extract over the ice ring in a punch bowl. Stir and pour in the sparkling wine. Serve in punch cups. Garnish each drink with an orange wheel.

JEREMIAH BLAKE
NASHVILLE, TENNESSEE

TIP *If you have extra time, Blake recommends making the ice for this punch from the same orange-spice tea used in the tea syrup. That way, as the ice melts, the drink remains perfectly flavorful.*

ORANGE-SPICE BLACK TEA SYRUP

MAKES ABOUT 1½ CUPS

1 cup granulated sugar

1 cup water

4 orange-spice black tea bags

❄ Heat the sugar and water in a medium saucepan over medium heat, stirring occasionally, until the sugar has dissolved. Add the tea bags, remove from the heat, and steep for 10 minutes. Remove the tea bags and let the syrup cool. Transfer to a clean glass bottle, cover, and refrigerate for up to 1 week.

CHAPTER 4

SEASONAL
Sips

Apples, pears, cranberries, citrus, and spices aplenty—these are the makings of a season full of merriment. And when it comes to the holidays, bartenders love to go all out, highlighting the best of winter's bounty to create drinks that are packed with seasonal flavors. From a Cranberry Smash (page 92) to a Kumquat-Cardamom Sidecar (page 82), these recipes will carry you through every wintry occasion, beginning with Thanksgiving and ending with New Year's Eve. Best of all? Most of these cocktails feature ingredients that you probably already have on hand for your holiday cooking.

YOU'LL SHOOT YOUR EYE OUT

Bold and bright, this lighthearted cocktail boasts a double dose of cinnamon, thanks to a spiced syrup and the cinnamon-forward Czech liqueur Becherovka—both complementing the deep richness of a generous pour of aged rum and the soft herbal notes of Bénédictine. "It's perfect for a cold winter night spent cozied up on the couch, watching a holiday flick," says San Francisco bartender Mathias Simonis, "which is what I pictured when I named the drink after the famous scene in *A Christmas Story*."

SERVES

1

TOOLS

mixing glass, barspoon, strainer

GLASS

coupe or rocks

GARNISH

orange twist

2 ounces aged rum

½ ounce Becherovka

½ ounce Bénédictine

¼ ounce Toasted Cinnamon Syrup (page 78)

3 dashes of Angostura orange bitters

Ice cubes

1 large ice cube (if using a rocks glass)

❄ Combine the rum, Becherovka, Bénédictine, cinnamon syrup, and bitters in a mixing glass. Add ice and stir until chilled. Strain into a coupe glass or over the large ice cube in a rocks glass. Garnish with the orange twist.

MATHIAS SIMONIS
TRICK DOG AND BON VIVANTS, SAN FRANCISCO, CALIFORNIA

TOASTED CINNAMON SYRUP

MAKES 1½ CUPS

1½ cups Simple Syrup (page 13)   5 cinnamon sticks

❄ In a small saucepan, warm the simple syrup over low heat. In a small skillet, toast the cinnamon sticks over medium heat until you smell their aroma, 3 to 5 minutes. Remove the cinnamon sticks from the heat and add to the simple syrup. Bring the syrup and cinnamon to a boil, then remove from the heat and set aside to cool. Strain into a clean glass bottle, cover, and refrigerate for up to 2 weeks.

TIP *If you don't feel like making your own cinnamon syrup, you can find many bottled versions, such as the one from B.G. Reynolds, which will work just as well.*

BRANDIED APPLE

What says "holiday" more than homemade apple pie? If you're bartender Erick Castro, that would be a spiced apple cocktail! In creating this recipe, Castro was inspired by the comforting flavors of apple pie, down to a dusting of cinnamon for a garnish. "I wanted to emulate the flavors, without making it overly sweet," he says. "It's a spiced cider in cocktail form." A light hand with the simple syrup and a balancing dose of fresh lemon juice keep the flavor of the apple cider clean and crisp, while Cognac adds just the right amount of warmth to this crowd-pleasing cocktail.

2 ounces Cognac

1 ounce fresh apple cider

½ ounce fresh lemon juice

½ ounce Simple Syrup (page 13)

Ice cubes

Combine the Cognac, cider, lemon juice, and simple syrup in a cocktail shaker. Add ice and shake well. Strain into a chilled sour glass and garnish with a dusting of cinnamon.

ERICK CASTRO
POLITE PROVISIONS, SAN DIEGO, CALIFORNIA

TIP *Castro says a fresh-pressed apple cider works best for flavor. Look for the unfiltered versions, which are commonly available around the holidays.*

SERVES

1

TOOLS

cocktail shaker, strainer

GLASS

sour

GARNISH

ground cinnamon

FALLING LEAVES

The fall and winter months in Michigan mean only one thing to Detroit bartender Rick Lane: a trip to the local cider mill. "Every visit was flavored with fresh cider, crisp apples, and warm doughnuts sprinkled with cinnamon and sugar," says Lane, "and I wanted to create a cocktail that would capture those cider mill days." With vodka serving as a blank boozy slate, fresh apple flavors intermingle with a squeeze of lemon and a splash of sweet syrup and bitters. Just remember to garnish with thin apple slices, a dusting of ground cinnamon, "and an extra dose of holiday cheer!" Lane says.

1½ ounces vodka

½ ounce fresh lemon juice

½ ounce Demerara Syrup
(recipe follows)

3 dashes of Angostura bitters

Ice cubes

1 ounce fresh apple cider

❋ Combine the vodka, lemon juice, syrup, and bitters in a cocktail shaker. Add ice and shake well. Strain into an ice-filled rocks glass, top with the cider, and garnish with the apple slice and a dusting of cinnamon.

RICK LANE
ROAST, DETROIT, MICHIGAN

DEMERARA SYRUP

MAKES ABOUT ¾ CUP

½ cup water

½ cup Demerara sugar

❋ Combine the water and sugar in a small saucepan and bring to a boil over medium-high heat. Turn the heat to medium-low and simmer, stirring slowly, until the sugar is dissolved, 2 to 3 minutes. Remove from the heat and let cool to room temperature. Transfer to a clean glass bottle, cover, and refrigerate for up to 2 weeks.

SERVES

1

TOOLS

cocktail shaker, strainer

GLASS

rocks

GARNISH

thin apple slice and ground cinnamon

SERVES

1

TOOLS

cocktail
shaker,
strainer

GLASS

coupe

GARNISH

fresh
kumquat
and freshly
grated
nutmeg

KUMQUAT-CARDAMOM SIDECAR

The tiny kumquat makes up in flavor for what it lacks in size, delivering a subtle citrus snap in this cardamom-spiced riff on the classic Sidecar. Infused with the cardamom and kumquats, white wine amps up the festive flavors while helping the cocktail maintain its lower-proof profile. "Cardamom and kumquat are such versatile flavors, capable of being either sweet or savory," says the cocktail's co-creator Doug Williams, "making this cocktail the perfect transition between lamb chops and holiday fruitcake."

1½ ounces Cognac

1½ ounces Kumquat-and-Cardamom-Infused White Wine (facing page)

½ ounce fresh lemon juice

½ ounce Simple Syrup (page 13)

Ice cubes

Combine the Cognac, infused wine, lemon juice, and simple syrup in a cocktail shaker. Add ice and shake well. Strain into a sugar-rimmed coupe and garnish with the fresh kumquat skewered on a cocktail pick and a dusting of nutmeg.

DOUG WILLIAMS AND STEPHEN LANDISH
THE HOTEL FOSTER AND BOONE & CROCKETT, MILWAUKEE, WISCONSIN

KUMQUAT-AND-CARDAMOM-INFUSED WHITE WINE

MAKES ABOUT 3¼ CUPS

1 (750-ml) bottle white wine
   (Pinot Grigio works well)

½ cup granulated sugar

24 kumquats, quartered

15 green cardamom pods

2 ounces vodka

❄ Combine the wine, sugar, kumquats, and cardamom pods in a large glass container. Cover and set aside to infuse for 24 hours. Strain into a clean glass bottle and add the vodka. Cover and refrigerate for up to 2 weeks.

(TIP) *Having a hard time finding kumquats? Navel oranges will also do the trick. Simply substitute the zest (no white pith) of 3 large oranges for the kumquats and infuse the wine as directed.*

The infused wine makes a delicious aperitif—just pour over ice and serve.

CLEMENTINE-PISCO COLLINS

SERVES

1

TOOLS

cocktail
shaker,
strainer

GLASS

Collins

GARNISH

clementine
wheel

Clementines are full of wintertime cheer, and this pisco-spiked cocktail from San Francisco bartender Maxine Sharkey Giammo wraps the seasonal citrus in a blanket of warming spice. A grape brandy native to wine-making areas in Chile and Peru, pisco is imbued with subtle notes of fruit and flowers, making it the perfect spirit to play up the other ingredients in this drink. "The spiced syrup and citrus give a fun seasonal twist to the floral notes of pisco," says Giammo, "and the floating pomegranate seeds add a pop of color, looking like Christmas lights bobbing in the shaker."

1½ ounces pisco

¾ ounce fresh lemon juice

½ ounce Clementine-Spiced Syrup (page 86)

4 segments of spiced clementines, reserved from the syrup

1 teaspoon fresh pomegranate seeds

Ice cubes

1½ ounces ginger beer

❄ Combine the pisco, lemon juice, spiced syrup, clementine segments, and pomegranate seeds in a cocktail shaker. Add ice and shake well. Strain into an ice-filled Collins glass, top with the ginger beer, and garnish with the clementine wheel.

MAXINE SHARKEY GIAMMO
HOG & ROCKS, SAN FRANCISCO, CALIFORNIA

TIP *Turn this single-serving cocktail into a party-ready punch by combining 1 (750-ml) bottle of pisco with 2½ cups of fresh lemon juice and 1¾ cups of the spiced syrup, and freeze overnight. The mixture will turn slightly slushy, which will help you keep the punch cold without needing to add ice to the bowl. An hour before the party, place the frozen mix in a punch bowl and add 3¾ cups of ginger beer, the seeds of 1 whole pomegranate, and all the syrup-soaked clementine segments. Ladle into ice-filled punch glasses and serve.*

CLEMENTINE-SPICED SYRUP

MAKES ABOUT 3 CUPS

2 cups granulated sugar

2 cups water

2 tablespoons grated clementine zest,
plus 6 fresh clementines, peeled
and separated into segments

1 (2-inch) piece of fresh ginger,
peeled and coarsely chopped

1 tablespoon whole allspice berries

1 tablespoon black peppercorns

1 tablespoon distilled white vinegar

Combine the sugar, water, clementine zest, ginger, allspice, and pepper-corns in a medium saucepan and bring to a boil. Lower the heat and simmer, stirring occasionally, until the sugar is dissolved. Remove from the heat, add the vinegar, and let cool to room temperature. Strain the syrup into a clean glass bottle and add the fresh clementine segments. Cover and refrigerate overnight or for up to 1 week.

SLEIGH RIDE

Setting out milk and cookies for Santa? Secure your spot on his "good" list this year with this mix of vodka, simple syrup, and an herbal Italian liqueur. "Milk adds such a creamy texture to cocktails," says Eric Johnson, partner at Sycamore Den in San Diego. "So it's perfect to reach for during the chillier months of the holiday season." Served tall over ice with a fresh grating of nutmeg, Johnson's Sleigh Ride is just the thing to help wash down a bellyful of peppermint patties and chocolate crinkles.

1 ounce vodka

1 ounce Galliano (see Tip)

¾ ounce Simple Syrup (page 13)

4 ounces milk

Dash of allspice dram

Ice cubes

Combine the vodka, Galliano, simple syrup, milk, and allspice dram in a cocktail shaker. Add ice and shake well. Strain into an ice-filled highball glass and garnish with a dusting of nutmeg.

ERIC JOHNSON
SYCAMORE DEN, SAN DIEGO, CALIFORNIA

TIP *Galliano—a vibrant, honey-hued herbal liqueur—dates back to late-nineteenth-century Italy. It is probably best known for its role (alongside vodka and orange juice) in the Harvey Wallbanger cocktail. Rich with notes of vanilla, anise, ginger, and even lavender, it's also delicious splashed into an afternoon cup of coffee or tea.*

SERVES

1

TOOLS

cocktail shaker, strainer

GLASS

highball

GARNISH

freshly grated nutmeg

GIBRALTAR

It's no secret that Texans have an affinity for tequila, but when the holidays roll around, locals often reach for tequila's smoky cousin, mezcal. It is similar to tequila, which is not surprising, since both are made from the agave plant. In mezcal production, the piña (or agave heart) is baked underground in wood-fired pits, imparting a distinct smokiness to the finished spirit. For San Antonio bar owner Jeret Pena, a quick mezcal rinse is all it takes to wrap his rich, seasonal sipper in a sultry blanket of warmth. "Smoke, apple, and pear are an amazing combo," says Pena, "especially in winter."

SERVES

1

TOOLS

cocktail
shaker,
strainer

GLASS

coupe or
cocktail

¼ ounce mezcal

1½ ounces Calvados

¾ ounce pear liqueur

½ ounce fresh lemon juice

¼ ounce Simple Syrup (page 13)

Ice cubes

Rinse a chilled coupe with the mezcal (see Tip). Combine the Calvados, pear liqueur, lemon juice, and simple syrup in a cocktail shaker. Add ice and shake well. Strain into a coupe.

JERET PENA
THE BROOKLYNITE, SAN ANTONIO, TEXAS

TIP *To "rinse" the glass, add the mezcal and swirl it around, making sure it reaches all the way up to the rim of the glass. Turn the glass upside down over a sink and give several quick taps to discard any remaining liquid.*

FIGGY TONIC

Forget the figgy pudding from the classic Christmas carol—this holiday season our taste buds are singing a different tune. Specifically, one of aged rum, port, and muddled dried figs. "I tried to think of what flavors would go with the old English dessert," says Charleston bartender Jackson Holland. "Both rum and port seemed a natural fit, and the tonic turns the drink into something spritzy that you can sip throughout a holiday gathering." Sounds like music to our ears.

2 dried figs, coarsely chopped

¼ ounce tawny port

¼ ounce fresh lemon juice

2 ounces aged rum

¼ ounce Simple Syrup (page 13)

Ice cubes

4 ounces tonic water

Combine the figs, port, and lemon juice in a cocktail shaker and gently muddle. Add the rum, simple syrup, and ice and shake well. Double strain into an ice-filled Collins glass, top with the tonic, and garnish with the skewered lemon wheel and fig slice.

JACKSON HOLLAND
THE COCKTAIL CLUB, CHARLESTON, SOUTH CAROLINA

TIP *Can't find dried figs? Swap in a heaping 1 tablespoon of fig preserves instead—just be sure to taste before adding the simple syrup. You may want to add less.*

SERVES

1

TOOLS

cocktail
shaker,
muddler,
strainer

GLASS

rocks

GARNISH

3 fresh
cran-
berries,
rosemary
sprig

CRANBERRY SMASH

A double dose of cranberries—both fresh and infused into the gin—finds its way into this seasonal smash, which picks up a subtle, savory note from the fresh rosemary. While many cocktails call for citrus juice and simple syrup, Detroit bar owner David Kwiatkowski suggests muddling diced lemon with sugar to extract essential oils from the peel. "The drink is like a bouquet of wintry flavors," says Kwiatkowski, "and it's green and red, which is a festive bonus."

1 sprig fresh rosemary

6 fresh cranberries

1 teaspoon Demerara sugar

¼ lemon, diced

2 ounces Cranberry-Infused Gin (facing page)

Ice cubes

1 large ice cube

Combine the rosemary, cranberries, sugar, and lemon in a cocktail shaker and muddle. Add the infused gin and ice and shake well. Strain over the large ice cube into a rocks glass and garnish with the 3 cranberries skewered on the rosemary sprig.

DAVID KWIATKOWSKI
SUGAR HOUSE, DETROIT, MICHIGAN

TIP *Since lemons vary in sweetness and acidity, consider having some simple syrup and fresh lemon juice on hand to adjust the cocktail's sweetness or tartness to suit your taste.*

CRANBERRY-INFUSED GIN

MAKES ABOUT 3 CUPS

1 (750-ml) bottle dry gin

1 cup fresh cranberries,
gently muddled

 Combine the gin and cranberries in a quart-size jar. Cover and let macerate for 1 week at room temperature. Strain into a clean glass bottle, cover, and store at room temperature for up to 1 year.

CHAPTER 5

Festive
SPARKLERS

Winter is the season for gathering to toast friends, family, good food, and all the best that life has to offer. Of course, it's not a toast without a little sparkle in your glass. Bubbly cocktails are the quintessential holiday sippers. After all, nothing welcomes your guests or celebrates an occasion quite like a flute of something effervescent. To top it off, sparkling cocktails are often lower in alcohol than their nonfizzy cousins—an extra bonus for holiday entertaining. From Northern Lights (a cranberry-and-gin-spiked sparkler; page 101) to Winter's Waltz (a blend of Aperol, pomegranate juice, and sparkling wine; page 106), these recipes will add a little pop to your parties.

ST. KNUT'S DAY

"In Scandinavia, St. Knut's Day marks the end of the Christmas season," explains Portland, Oregon, bartender Dave Shenaut. "Christmas trees are taken down, and a tradition similar to trick-or-treating is observed— adults and children go door-to-door to their neighbors' homes and are invited in for festive snacks and alcoholic beverages." As an homage to that tradition, Shenaut created this sparkling cocktail, which is perfect for ringing in the New Year.

1 ounce aquavit

½ ounce honey syrup (2:1; see Note on page 42)

¾ ounce fresh lemon juice

2 dashes of Peychaud's bitters

Ice cubes

3 ounces cold prosecco

❄ Combine the aquavit, honey syrup, lemon juice, and bitters in a cocktail shaker. Add ice and shake well. Strain into a chilled coupe, top with the prosecco, and garnish with the lemon twist and star anise.

DAVE SHENAUT
RAVEN & ROSE, PORTLAND, OREGON

SERVES

1

TOOLS

cocktail shaker, strainer

GLASS

coupe or flute

GARNISH

lemon twist, whole star anise

SERVES

1

TOOLS

cocktail
shaker,
strainer

GLASS

flute

GARNISH

lemon twist

MERRY ROSE

"I wanted to create a simple, floral, Champagne-style cocktail, so I did a twist on the French 75," says Australian bartender Michael Enright of this recipe's inspiration. Of course, Australians celebrate Christmas and New Year's in their warmer months of the year, but no matter the season, this cocktail remains perfectly versatile and festive. It's a great option for a before- or after-dinner drink, or as a cocktail for toasting the New Year.

1 ounce London dry gin

¼ ounce rose syrup, such as Monin

½ ounce fresh lemon juice

Ice cubes

4 ounces cold sparkling wine

Combine the gin, rose syrup, and lemon juice in a cocktail shaker. Add ice and shake well. Strain into a flute and top with the sparkling wine. Garnish with the lemon twist.

MICHAEL ENRIGHT
THE BARBER SHOP, SYDNEY, AUSTRALIA

JASMINE SMILES

Ted Kilgore was looking for something light and easy to pair with a seafood brunch, when he remembered fellow bartender Paul Harrington's Jasmine cocktail, which combined gin, Campari, Cointreau, and fresh lemon juice. "While I love the original, I wanted something lighter," he says. "Reducing the alcohol components and topping the drink with bubbles was exactly what it needed—still a Jasmine, but with a twinkle in her eye!" Best of all, the festive fizzer lends itself to being made in advance, allowing you to serve a delicious drink and mingle at your own cocktail party.

SERVES

1

TOOLS

cocktail
shaker,
strainer

GLASS

flute

GARNISH

flamed
orange peel
(optional,
see Tip)

½ ounce gin

½ ounce Campari

½ ounce Cointreau

½ ounce fresh lemon juice

Ice cubes

4 ounces brut sparkling wine

Combine the gin, Campari, Cointreau, and lemon juice in a cocktail shaker. Add ice and shake well. Strain into a flute and top with the sparkling wine. Garnish with the flamed orange peel, if desired.

TED KILGORE
PLANTERS HOUSE, ST. LOUIS, MISSOURI

TIP *To flame an orange peel, cut a quarter-size piece of peel from an orange, including the zest and about half of the pith. Light a match and allow it to burn down to the wood. Hold the peel with the orange side facing down, several inches above the cocktail, and position the lit match between the cocktail and the zest. Give the zest a squeeze to ignite the oils. Drop the zest into the drink or discard it.*

Kilgore suggests making this drink in large batches for serving at parties. Simply measure 4 ounces of each liquid (except the sparkling wine), stir together in a pitcher or jar, and refrigerate for at least 2 hours. When you're ready to serve, stir the mixture again and fill each flute to about the one-third mark. Top with bubbly and let the party begin.

NORTHERN LIGHTS

This festive fizzer gets a saucy makeover thanks to several teaspoons of a favorite holiday condiment—just be sure to hold the turkey. "It's the perfect welcome drink at any holiday soirée," says Los Angeles bartender David Delaney. "It's light and refreshing, and who doesn't want to kick off the night with some bubbly?"

SERVES

1

TOOLS

cocktail shaker, strainer, fine-mesh strainer

GLASS

flute

GARNISH

3 fresh cranberries

1 ounce gin

½ ounce Simple Syrup (page 13)

½ ounce fresh lemon juice

2 teaspoons cranberry sauce

2 dashes of Angostura bitters

Ice cubes

2 ounces cold sparkling wine

❄ Combine the gin, simple syrup, lemon juice, cranberry sauce, and bitters in a cocktail shaker. Add ice and shake well. Double strain into a chilled flute and top with the sparkling wine. Garnish with the cranberries, skewered on a cocktail pick.

DAVID DELANEY
LOS ANGELES, CALIFORNIA

SERVES

1

TOOLS

cocktail
shaker,
strainer,
fine-mesh
strainer

GLASS

flute

GARNISH

orange
twist

THE BROWN TURKEY

One bite of savory fig stuffing served at a holiday feast, and Austin bartender Justin Chamberlin knew he'd found his next cocktail inspiration. This formula combines the subtle spices of aged rum with the sultry sweetness of figs and a bright, bubbly pop of sparkling wine. "The dried fruit adds a deepness of flavor that plays well with the sparkling wine," says Chamberlin. "Of course, bubbles are a great match with any celebration, and figs spark an appetite for both food and holiday merriment."

1 ounce aged rum

1 ounce Fig and Brown Sugar
   Reduction (facing page)

3 dashes of orange bitters

Ice cubes

2 ounces cold sparkling wine

Combine the rum, fig reduction, and bitters in a cocktail shaker. Add ice and shake well. Double strain into a chilled flute, top with the sparkling wine, and garnish with the orange twist.

JUSTIN L. CHAMBERLIN
SAGRA, AUSTIN, TEXAS

FIG AND BROWN SUGAR REDUCTION

MAKES ABOUT 1 CUP

1 cup water

1 cup light brown sugar

½ cup chopped dried figs

❄ Combine the water and brown sugar in a medium saucepan over medium-high heat, stirring to dissolve the sugar. Add the dried figs and bring to a boil. Cover, remove from the heat, and let steep for 25 minutes. Double strain into a clean glass bottle, cover, and refrigerate for up to 2 weeks.

TIP *If your holiday plans call for a handful of houseguests, make a double batch of the fig reduction to have on hand for serving atop pancakes, waffles, or ice cream.*

EBENEZER SCROOGE

Feeling the bah-humbug blues? This cocktail from Seattle barman Kenaniah Bystrom turns one of the most bitter bar mixers, Cynar, into a supple holiday sipper. "At Essex we often use bitter liqueurs as the foundation for our drinks," Bystrom says. "So I started with Cynar for depth and balanced it out with ginger and brown sugar for spicy sweetness, lemon for brightness, and sparkling wine for a dry fizz."

1½ ounces Cynar (see Tip)

¾ ounce ginger liqueur (Bystrom uses Domaine de Canton)

½ ounce fresh lemon juice

1 teaspoon brown sugar

Dash of Angostura bitters

Ice cubes

2 ounces cold sparkling wine

Combine the Cynar, ginger liqueur, lemon juice, brown sugar, and bitters in a cocktail shaker. Add ice and shake well. Strain into a chilled flute, top with the sparkling wine, and garnish with a dusting of nutmeg.

KENANIAH BYSTROM
ESSEX, SEATTLE, WASHINGTON

TIP *Cynar (pronounced chee-nar) is an amaro, which is a bitter Italian liqueur. It's made from more than a dozen plants and botanicals, artichoke being the most predominant. But before you wrinkle your nose, know that it doesn't actually taste like the leafy thistle! Instead, Cynar is earthy and root-y with underlying chocolaty notes, which really come out when mixed with citrus. Aside from its Italian homeland, Cynar is especially popular in Switzerland, where locals mix it with orange juice.*

SERVES

1

TOOLS

cocktail shaker, strainer

GLASS

flute

GARNISH

freshly grated nutmeg

SERVES

1

TOOLS

barspoon

GLASS

flute

GARNISH

fresh pome-granate seeds or blood orange twist

WINTER'S WALTZ

The classic Aperol Spritz gets a wintry makeover in this seasonal sparkler from Los Angeles–based Matthew Biancaniello. Combining fresh, seasonal fruit with a low-proof Italian aperitif and a heady pour of sparkling wine, it's a great option for entertaining—simply set out the fruit juice, Aperol, and some bubbles on ice and let guests mix up their own spritz. "Just be sure to use the freshest, most fragrant fruit you can find," says Biancaniello, "and press the juice from the fruit right before you plan to start mixing."

¾ ounce Aperol

1 ounce fresh pomegranate or blood orange juice

4 ounces cold sparkling wine

In a chilled flute, combine the Aperol and fresh pomegranate juice and stir to combine. Top with the sparkling wine, gently stir again, and garnish with pomegranate seeds.

MATTHEW BIANCANIELLO
CLIFF'S EDGE, LOS ANGELES, CALIFORNIA

SANG ROYALE

Sparkling cocktails can be just as complex and lively as their bubble-free counterparts, as this beautifully layered drink shows. Kansas City bartender Ryan Maybee was thinking of Blood and Sand when he created the Sang Royale, inspired by that classic cocktail's combination of sweet vermouth and fruit juice. Sparkling wine brings the alcohol content down and gives the drink a welcome lightness.

SERVES

1

GLASS

flute

GARNISH

brandied
cherry

1 ounce Byrrh (see Tip) or sweet
   vermouth

¾ ounce cold fresh grapefruit juice

2 dashes of Angostura bitters

4 ounces cold brut sparkling wine

Pour the Byrrh, grapefruit juice, and bitters into a chilled flute. Top with the sparkling wine and garnish with the brandied cherry.

RYAN MAYBEE
MANIFESTO, KANSAS CITY, MISSOURI

TIP A French wine–based aperitif, Byrrh has only recently become widely available in the United States, though it dates back to the 1860s, when it was originally invented as a way to make quinine palatable to soldiers and colonials who were living in malaria-ridden outposts. These days, it is mostly enjoyed for its delicious, lightly herbal flavor and its cocktail-friendly qualities. If you spring for a bottle to make this cocktail, don't fret if you have a lot left over. Simply enjoy it as the French do—chilled and, if you like, with a small slice of lemon. It makes a perfect holiday aperitif.

CZECH 75

"During the holiday season, I lean toward darker spirits, and apple brandy works great here," says Vancouver bartender Shaun Layton. A splash of the Czech-born liqueur Becherovka introduces flavors of cinnamon and clove, while the citrus and bitters add complexity and balance, and the sparkling wine gives the drink length and texture. "I think one—or three—of these before a nice holiday dinner would be a grand idea," adds Layton.

1 ounce applejack

½ ounce Becherovka

⅓ ounce Simple Syrup (page 13)

1 ounce fresh lemon juice

2 dashes of Angostura bitters

Ice cubes

2½ ounces cold sparkling wine

Combine the applejack, Becherovka, simple syrup, lemon juice, and bitters in a cocktail shaker. Add ice and shake well. Strain into a chilled flute, top with the sparkling wine, and garnish with the lemon twist.

SHAUN LAYTON
L'ABATTOIR, VANCOUVER, BRITISH COLUMBIA

TIP *Turn this sparkling sipper into a warming toddy! Simply swap in hot water for the sparkling wine, combine all the ingredients in a mug, and stir.*

SERVES

1

TOOLS

cocktail shaker, strainer

GLASS

flute

GARNISH

long lemon twist

HOLIDAY ENTERTAINING TIPS & TRICKS

Holiday entertaining can be overwhelming, but it doesn't have to be that way.
Here are some of our favorite tips and tricks for ensuring stress-free festivities.

THE BIG CHILL

Ice rings can be essential when it comes to making punches. Fortunately, they're a cinch to make. Simply fill a Bundt pan with water and freeze the day before you're planning to serve. It's a good idea to freeze two so that you have a backup. And be sure to set the pans on a level surface in the freezer so the water freezes evenly. To get the frozen mold out of the ring, just run some water over the ice, and then carefully turn the pan upside down while supporting the ice ring.

JOIN THE PARTY

If you're hosting a party, don't forget to enjoy yourself! That means you shouldn't be playing bartender all night. Unless you're a bartending dynamo, making dozens of cocktails and being a good host at the same time is virtually impossible. Here are a few ideas for planning that will allow you to have a good time at your own party:

• Ask a friend to make drinks at your party in exchange for bar duty at his or her fête.

• Before the party, squeeze fresh juices and prep syrups (and any other ingredients you can) to save time later on.

• Make punches ahead of time and let guests serve themselves.

• Grate spices and make citrus peels for garnishes ahead of time, so they're ready to go when it's time to pour your drinks.

GLASS ACT

If spending money on matching sets of the right glassware stresses you out, think about going vintage and mixing and matching styles. Your local Goodwill store carries loads of fun and inexpensive glassware, and don't be afraid to get creative with whatever you already have around. (See page 114 for information about the different types of glassware used in this book.)

TAXI!

As a host, you always want to plan for safe departures for your guests. Make sure everyone has a designated driver and print out a list of cabbie phone numbers to post near the door or hand to guests as they prepare to leave.

PARTY FAVORS

Looking for a fun way to make sure friends remember your party? Laminate recipe cards for the cocktails you will serve and give them to guests as they leave.

CHILL OUT

Lots of holiday cocktails call for sparkling wine as a key ingredient. Since you never shake sparkling wine with the rest of your ingredients, be sure to chill your wine ahead of time so it keeps the cocktails nice and cool once you pour it in.

CRACKING UP

Shaking up egg cocktails like the Spice Nog Flip (page 31) or the Añejo Tequila and Amontillado Sherry Eggnog (page 33)? Crack the egg into a small ramekin or bowl before adding it to the shaker to avoid accidentally mixing in any errant bits of shell. Also, make sure your eggs are super-fresh and feel free to go with pasteurized eggs if you're uneasy about mixing with raw ones.

SHARE THE WEALTH

Making lots of cocktails or big batches of punch can be expensive, so consider hosting a potluck where guests are assigned to bring certain spirits instead of snacks.

BOTTLE SHOP

If you're planning to batch a bunch of cocktails in advance and you don't have enough containers to hold all of the mixtures, simply reuse the empty bottles that held the spirits.

COOL LIKE THAT

You never want to run out of ice in the middle of a party, so make sure you've made or bought plenty of ice for your drinks. You can store it in coolers and use it as needed.

TOOL TIME

Be sure to have on hand all of the tools you'll need to make your cocktails—plenty of shakers, barspoons, muddlers, and strainers. Ask friends ahead of time if you need to borrow their tools, so you're sure to be fully outfitted when you're ready to start mixing.

JUICY FRUIT

You'll likely use a lot of citrus juice in your holiday drinks, so you'll want to get as much juice out of the fruit as possible. To do this, be sure to store your citrus at room temperature, and when you're ready to juice them, first roll them under your hand on a counter surface. This will release the juices within the fruit so that when you cut into them, they're ready to release every last drop.

SPICE IS NICE

Holiday cocktails are chock-full of wintry spice, and to maximize the flavor factor, you'll want to use the freshest whole spices possible (throw out that decades-old container of ground cinnamon already!). Crush or grate them at the last minute for nuanced cocktails with layers of fresh seasonal spice. (Consider investing in a mortar and pestle or a Microplane grater—even a few spins in a clean coffee grinder would do the trick.)

BECOME A MUDDLE MASTER

Many cocktails that call for fresh herbs, citrus, or spice will instruct you to muddle the ingredients before shaking in order to release added aromas and flavors. But pulverize the ingredients into a pulp and the drink can take on unwanted bitter notes (not to mention extra floaties). Instead, gently press the ingredients with the muddler into the bottom or side of the cocktail shaker, give a slight twist, and repeat—five times ought to do it.

GLASSWARE

Before the holidays, you'll want to pull out the special glassware you've put in storage for the year. Or perhaps you plan to purchase new glassware to supplement your collection so that you'll be able to serve a large crowd. The following is a list of the different types of glassware used in this book. If you don't have the specific glass called for in the recipe you're making, don't be afraid to substitute another with a similar shape.

❄

BRANDY SNIFTER: A short-stemmed glass with a wide, bulbous bowl and a relatively narrow mouth, which helps capture aromas.

COCKTAIL: A V-shaped glass with a long stem, also known as a Martini glass, which is designed to serve "up" drinks and keep warm fingers away from the cold liquid.

COLLINS: A tall 8- to 14-ounce glass that is often used for iced drinks and those with carbonated ingredients, as its slender design helps to retain the drink's fizz.

CORDIAL: A petite 1- to 3-ounce glass used for aperitifs and digestifs, as well as for small cocktails.

COUPE: A stemmed, saucer-shaped 4- to 8-ounce glass often used for classic cocktails and drinks made with sparkling wine.

FLUTE: A tall, stemmed 6- to 10-ounce glass designed to keep Champagne bubbly; it is also used for cocktails with sparkling wine.

GOBLET: A stemmed glass with a rounded bowl; often interchangeable with a wineglass.

HIGHBALL: Larger than a rocks glass but shorter than a Collins, this glass is most often used for drinks with cubed or cracked ice and carbonated ingredients.

IRISH COFFEE: Also known as a toddy glass, this tall 8- to 12-ounce mug is usually footed and has a handle to protect hands from the hot liquid.

JUICE: A small glass cup with a 4- to 5-ounce capacity.

MUG: A glass or ceramic cup with a handle, which is usually used for serving hot drinks; mugs with a 6- to 8-ounce capacity are best for cocktails.

OLD-FASHIONED: *See* Rocks.

PUNCH CUP: A small glass cup, often with a handle, that is used for serving cold or hot drinks.

ROCKS: Also known as an old-fashioned glass, this 6- to 8-ounce short, round glass is used for holding ice and spirits, as well as some cocktails, most notably the Old Fashioned.

SOUR: This 4- to 6-ounce stemmed glass that tapers slightly at the bottom is the classic choice for serving a Whiskey Sour.

TEACUP: A small cup with a handle and usually a saucer, which is used to serve hot drinks.

TODDY: *See* Irish Coffee.

INDEX

LIQUID MEASUREMENTS

Barspoon	=	1 teaspoon
1 teaspoon	=	⅙ ounce
1 tablespoon	=	½ ounce
2 tablespoons (pony)	=	1 ounce
3 tablespoons (jigger)	=	1½ ounces
¼ cup	=	2 ounces
⅓ cup	=	3 ounces
½ cup	=	4 ounces
⅔ cup	=	5 ounces
¾ cup	=	6 ounces
1 cup	=	8 ounces
1 pint	=	16 ounces
1 quart	=	32 ounces
750 ml bottle	=	25.4 ounces
1 liter bottle	=	33.8 ounces